HEAT, SOB, LILY

HEAT, SOB, LILY

Kristina Andersson Bicher

MadHat Press
Cheshire, Massachusetts

MadHat Press
MadHat Incorporated
PO Box 422, Cheshire, MA 01225

Copyright © 2025 Kristina Andersson Bicher
All rights reserved.

The Library of Congress has assigned
this edition a Control Number of
2024948750

ISBN 978-1-952335-90-7 (paperback)

Words by Kristina Andersson Bicher
Cover image: *Lily Fairy* by Falero Luis Ricardo, 1888
Cover design by Marc Vincenz

www.MadHat-Press.com

First Printing
Printed in the United States of America

Table of Contents

I.

Girl /	3
Says Daughter /	5
Girl Learns to Speak /	6
Rendered Human /	7
Grandmother's Advice /	8
Neighbor Girl to Mrs. G /	9
Recall /	11
Midwinter/Penance /	14
Open Window /	15
After the War /	16
Latin Quarter /	17
Rebel Bride /	18
When we split, oh how /	19
Apology for a Lost Dog /	20
How to Survive a Shipwreck /	21
Joseph's Annunciation /	22

II.

Winter, I Fell /	25
Glider Plane /	26
Mothercake /	28
In Minneapolis (where you learn a new word) /	29
In the News /	30
Chronicles of Lazarus /	32
The Lazarus Files /	35
Credo /	36
Locked In /	37
When He Calls /	39
Refractory /	40
Loving Lazarus /	42

On the Island Where Venus / 44
Aftermath / 45

III.

Young Carl Jung / 49
More to Say / 51
In Amsterdam, Waiting / 52
Undressed / 53
New Year's Eve / 54
Desire / 55
Love Is a Rebel Bird / 56
Her Ambivalence / 61
Mannequins / 62

IV.

Ars Poetica / 67
The First Time I Saw Jesus / 68
How to Get Divorced / 70
On Boxing Day / 72
The Book of Hope / 73
Criss-Crossed / 77
That Night Jack Wanted Me / 78
In Bed in the Country / 79
In New York / 80
When I Say I Love Art, I Mean / 84
An Insomniac to Her Men / 85
They Will Enter / 86
Birth / 88

Acknowledgments 89
About the Author 91

I.

Girl

Girl squanders her fish sticks
   beats her gums against
                      monoliths

She
   is a gifted bootlicker
her bootlicking is prolific— *Father LOOK*
    our Girl is a
phenom! Let us toast to her Very Promising Future

her parents feed her
       an enormous chain
she burps gold and they are stung with glee
      when she spits tin, she's cold-
           shouldered

Girl flips her feathers everywhere
      (to herself: I will join the Spoonbill Revolution — I
   will be Lead Tanager)

Dear, cautions Father, you cannot eat air— *Oh Daddy,*
you're dead, remember?

Doll, says Mother, let us scrub
         the sour from your soul   *please Mother-may-you*

Kristina Andersson Bicher

then Girl is a BAD butterfly

Her kleptocracy hits the skids
    she is shook
        by cops
       till her tinsel falls
   [purloined necklace   dime store ring]

o haven't we ... haven't we   her parents clock
their heads together

Says Daughter

    (a golden shovel after Franz Wright)

Mother, I see you: a child tied to a tree and
your mother batting your rag doll off the sill when
she knew your bloom would eclipse her. She who was
always screaming, screaming till she was burnt from it. And the
dark rain fell. You grew, an oak no one could lash. At last
swam an ocean to get away. Though still a girl, in time
met a man and raised your own flesh to crown. With
beds unmade and scolds to scold. So genuine
your love for these new mouths, fresh-filling with sorrow,
though you vowed to stack that rage in your spine and
house it ever there. Still unseen it grew, longing
to crush what your hand would touch. How you ached to
banish those phantoms childhood bred. So to change
what would not yield, to dredge those stones you
were fed with a spoon. Tell me, Mother, how you got
this far and who you had to bury. On
my table, you are laid. Sunk in my mouth, your
cry, on my legs your bent and sturdy knees.

Kristina Andersson Bicher

Girl Learns to Speak

reach
    down   the dark
                of her throat

        tear out the ball
    the boat   the bird
           and the brick

a wave rushes
            ungripped

    her voice   reedy pushing
                  its note

Rendered Human

Each time my mother birthed she bled. Bled
such that on any given bygone day
we might have been her assassins.

I say this so you understand depletion (pints
and pints, we were given to know)
and from what stone halls we rose.

The first arrived in ice, the second into bells. I emptied
out of a ruby storm: bramble-swaddled, fed
sumac from a spoon. We, exiled,

lived outdoors as mice. Say wild wooded
things rattling the leaf bin, sun-razored, blanched
blue. In time we took on the coolness

of toads. Mother churning in the quiet factory
of her face. When humans turn to totems
longing curls the tongue. It took a

violent ache, a hard blow to wake
me into being. Thank you broken
plates. The shock and shriek

that opened from my mouth, some elemental
iron climbing up my throat.

Kristina Andersson Bicher

Grandmother's Advice

child, she says   there will come a man
who tugs your rings   tongues each finger
base to tip   breaks the lace
at your collarbone   curves his lips
and sets free the pearl   spine of buttons
slips his way down   then splits you open
not always blossomsweet   but breathbrute
and hands like vines   into your half-sprung heart
make room   for his ransom
the corset will   come back for you
days and days of ice   white nights

Neighbor Girl to Mrs. G

Lady   your wedding band on the counter rung
clear and river-like   I was rushed
to motion   chucked it in the thicket   flushed
it down the toilet   my pocket   ate it
put it back on its porcelain mountaintop   I don't
remember   but tell me

if you cry at night and no one comforts   wake
if you say   nothing   being   animal   if you suck
blood from your own cuts   what   what
grows then

I'm dirty Lady   my fingers squeeze
green poppy buds   pry out seeds
lick the milk-glue   worms I scrape
and pinch from soil   my nailbeds
stain black

I don't remember
your face   I like to think now   you were old
no longer needing brassy things   maybe I dreamed
never stole   maybe one day you came
to me saying *see here darlin' girl see here   something*
and it's just for you

I don't know my own face
Mother washed it so I never had to
look at me   I know the first sin seeds
the hunger   I had married   just married and took

that other man   I don't remember
his face   but he wore   and I

O the muck   Lady I grow weeds

Recall

how medallions multiplied across that childhood rug
fluid acres weft from silk worms, deep plush muzzling the floors,
ornamental, dazzling, how stains darken with time, rugs and
    how we cross them, leave the crushmarks of our feet

there were closets and doors: how the air stilled when you
    shut them. Sawdusted
drawers with knobs like little shells or jewels or talismans, the
    tiny boxes little girls
obsess over, the miniature dolls buried within

a memory of hands, of fingers spread wide or clasped or clawing
    or reaching skyward
toward nothing at all, the terror of grown-ups, of long lifting
    arms, shoulders
that square the weight, bodies like tall trees, flagpoles, like
    wooden masts of ships

and houses, how they sweat with sun, creak with wind, how
    the field mice find holes
to enter, how in a dream you fall into a room hidden inside
    another room

how quiet the rooms are without parents, without other
    children or when any
one person is missing

mouths, how they hinge apart, unpurse to reveal soft pink
    caves and wet teeth

slippery tongues, how a person's whole face changes, how the
    weather changes
when the mouth moves, calls out in code and you see the
    animal living within

recall the moon, how it's made of gypsum, how poppies wilt in
    its light
how blankets can't cover both your feet and your face and you
    have to choose what
part of you will be cold, how dark branches scratch the skin of
    the house at night

how when one person yells, the other people in the room
    either shrink or grow
and the ones that grow get swollen and the ones that shrink,
    shrink into flowers
and drawer pulls and rug fringe and the buds on branch tips
    set to explode

how the ballerina is draped in baby blue satin and stiff folds of
    tulle, her calf muscles
lacquered, the small pearl of her chin, the metal thread that
    enters her big toe
to become her spine, the darkness where she lies, the quiet,
    the hinge, the turnkey

little wheels that grind in the dark, the whir beneath the skin,
    the animals buried
in dark boxes, sleeping dancers, coiled springs, beds of
    gypsum, satin moon, wilted

tongue, house of poppies, elaborate pronged coins that repeat
    and repeat and repeat

spreading stains, the large things that go unsaid, the terrible
    silence when the music
has yet to begin to play

Kristina Andersson Bicher

Midwinter / Penance

A woman sits at a kitchen table.
A man sits opposite.
He wears the face of indictment.
Between them smoke attaches to the pendant lamp.
Between them the table is a frozen lake.
Every morning he is there.
To fasten her hair shirt.
She lifts her arms.

Open Window

At night he comes to bed with angers
he has swallowed and when he sleeps

his grievances blister
branch in him like trees, each

twig and root forking smaller, forking
deeper until he's consumed. Left foot

clawing at the sheet. Just now
outside, rain chatters the sash

and sill. The sleep-sighs of leaves
slip in, slip out the open

window and fluster the lace. Husband:
do not wake

Kristina Andersson Bicher

After the War

I. Man (knotted)

having run out of   boat
nerved   disquiet
     fever sweeping
         into his mouth
here a man   at once threadlike   flutter
deep in the disappearing

II. Woman (nerved)

sweeping   out of   into   woman
    knotted   she threadlike
         mouths a fever
disquiet   at the deep flutter
   in their boat
    the everyday   disappearing
run   a woman once wrote

Latin Quarter

Here fallen, here felled. A dead-
end alley, a man, 1944. And now a café
where I fill myself with wine-soaked
beef. Chatter of forks on porcelain.
A wet-skinned goblet. The candle
gasps. *Ici est tombé.* Paris wrote his name
in marble. This city is a crypt, each
horse fresh-gilt. See how absence
remains. Bonnard left his wife
in the tub—see how she blues.

Kristina Andersson Bicher

Rebel Bride

Once a girl fed milkweed
to the clouds, padded
her petticoat with pearls
swept rice
off the moon   she

frosted her face
and sorted barnacles
from apple blooms
left the hominy   out

in a hard rain   salted
an igloo and poached
the scallops in a bath of glue

she tripped on her ghost
in a blizzard   cleaned
the cadaver with cotton
smoked a white flag   doused
the court order in lye

tossed yeast
upon the bones

When we split, oh how

that voice calved
        and howled
our bleached vow

        chide vowel

my white volt
        in a wilted cove

Kristina Andersson Bicher

Apology for a Lost Dog

For the inner weather of our house I am sorry
we'd gone deaf to you

We searched for you   in roadside ditches

What had we done   had we done   that year you kept escaping
first the trek to our old home (crossing highways) then the night
you leapt the stonewall   the waitress squealed her brakes

In heavy boots of winter we taped your face to every pole
     made known your name
to every cop and city sanitation crew

One January morning you didn't heed our calls   had run   fell
12 feet down into an open concrete basement
     8 days in that pit

Did you mean to flee?   *(I did)*
Was it so bad then?   *(It was)*

When the fireman   cradled your body up the metal rungs
offering   you shallow breath   when I ran to you when
you looked at me   hesitated

How to Survive a Shipwreck

after the 1972 film Poseidon Adventure

Preparation is everything! Pamela Sue, O the crimson gash
Of those crushed velvet hotpants waiting under your skirt.
Scamper up that tree in satin heels before the glass walls give
    and the inverted world fills and fills with cries and cold brine.
Every girl learns hotness is the hook but helpless is the reel.
I'm nothing, Gene Hackman, without you ... don't leave me!
Dowdy Shelley dies in granny panties; the hooker must burn.
O, Virgins of summer, are you just waiting to be found? Put down
    your fruit glosses and curling wands, pick up that pipe wrench,
Now pound your way free. The steel here's only one inch thick.

Kristina Andersson Bicher

Joseph's Annunciation

from the Mérode triptych of Robert Campin

I'm so ugly, Joseph says—

aloud, alone, all day
hatcheting wood, gyrating drill joints
sawdust leaping off saw teeth—

paper wall between him
and M, untouchable in carmine
her knee a burst, rhapsodic star—

he hears the thick beat
of archangel wings, the merchant
and his wife at the keyhole—

I am cuckold. Less than cuckold—

then a baby no bigger
than a tip of tongue, on a silver cross, in a spill
of light, slides down from clouds—

My life is over.

II.

Winter, I Fell

into grief, dropped my keys
in snow: they slipped
like oil into a mound
of brightness that would not hold
their falling. Not even
a gasp from the trees.

Kristina Andersson Bicher

Glider Plane

on his sixteenth birthday
we shot him into the ether—

(his arc still true)
slung him blue-ward   tossed

the baby up to see
if he could fly

those were the days before
fog ate the valley   before a boy
bit the moon and was diamond

he circled once   twice

three times   *(oh so weightless!)*

we stood on a field watching   rooted
among the dry stalks
chests full   faces wet with sun and we
held up that sky

we should never have exhaled

but grown   lengthened   yes   opened up   and out
into spruces sprouting ten thousand arms and each
with ten thousand fingers until we formed

a lush green net   a sieve   you see

HEAT, SOB, LILY

this was long
ago   when once   once
a small bird sang

Kristina Andersson Bicher

Mothercake

This is not a birthday for a son
not a table but an altar

This is not a knife but a sharp hand
The same that broke the eggs

She lights the petite torches
To see where the wind comes from

This is not a fire
But a light to remember his lashes by

In Minneapolis (where you learn a new word)

crying into your cream of wild rice soup sobbing with your mother on the phone in a coffee shop weeping the strange prognosis and hoping your sunglasses are dark enough   someone plunks a wad of napkins on the table in front of you and the napkins splay and flutter as they fall   you look up   a man with a long white beard and skin like an old sweet potato has given you this   says nothing and walks out the door   you're looking now at the picture window and suddenly a clown in tent stripes and blue wig waves at you   and behind him a dark smudge of a dog then a small human on a skateboard   you've forgotten your woe but still there are words one must try to avoid (*degenerative* and *refractory* are two)   your mother advises fresh air, moving the legs   you have sopped thru most of the napkins but stash the remainder in your tote   they are the color of unbleached wheat   outside the sun is blanching the bodies on the sidewalk and you go looking for a river   later over drinks you tell the story to K who says a poet creates her own idiom and then you know what you must do   you must fight for every scrap in the face of this   and is there such a thing as pre-grief   is it the same as preparation   is it like being grass-bound watching the undersides of clouds   now you've left this town   going home on a plane   you can stop your leaking   there's a big man next to you slumped on his tray-table   you want to tell him that it's ok to lean on you could he please lean on you

Kristina Andersson Bicher

In the News

+

another boy was gravely ill was gravely
ill he suffered so his suffering
was manifold his suffering was

manifold his suffering was manifold

+

and when he died his house came down
they stomped it down so no one
would remember him remember him

remember

+

did he toe-walk talk
to angels talk to no
one   Mother O
were there signs Mother
did you *miss*
the signs O

O—

+

had she wheeled
him through school halls or pricked
his pretty thumb   or thumped
his chest thrice daily   encased
his head in foam   had he a crooked gait
they would have forgiven her
her son

+

let this be a lesson not
to be born
with the wrong illness

+

the maze that was
his mind
was set
to blaze   the wires
tripped   the match
was lit
he got a gun
the suffering
was manifold

was manifold

Kristina Andersson Bicher

Chronicles of Lazarus

I. HE WHO IS NOW CALLED LAZARUS

was born a plain boy we
christened KRISTER
and thus it went

>   first his brain torqued then grew
>   claws and we
>   were sore afraid

AND so the born KRISTER waned and so a new corpus rose
like a mountain and lo, it would hold several dogs—
a sofa, pack of smokes and some broken remotes there were
guns in there too *(sore afraid)*

>   the worst plan became the only plan

>   we wet the dirt
>   with our faces, cracked
>   lips on broke hopes

KRISTER no more. But if we call out, "Lazarus!"
who is it that comes to us and who
will we be THEN
when we receive him?

II. THAT WEEK

For 3 days, shouting from the upstairs room. Behind the door: a TV and a man-child. Plates of picked-at pizza and hills of dishes rising through thorns of forks.

On the 4th day, food no longer looked human, brittled-dark on edges. Newspapers aged like teeth. The body smelled of need.

And still the blue-white light washed his cheeks and brow and bled from the crack under the door but he was gone.

On the 5th day, had he been able to speak, Lazarus might have said he was going on a journey. From which he …

When there was shouting, she longed for silence. When there was silence, her longing died. The 6th day.

On the 7th day, God rested his case.

III. WHAT CAME NEXT

cuts and wars and two by fours, it hungry see grow, chasm yawn and shine, fill maw add water, doctors, deities. chain smoke (add smoke) cold soak, all chok and stam. woman man plan, dogs, drinks kitchen sink, star-cross armor chinks. cicadas ghotsing up the tress, wees and circus, beaches, bawlig, twitches glitches, summer's tink. a blur of yleling, not tell, layers, crystal dishes. add car and darnk and blowsn away tired, dents and cops and dope. raging, hzay, pcing, voices, voices, then quiet. chains. lawyers in chairs.

The Lazarus Files

arrive: loose white
sheets in plain white
wrapper

she reads them like the weather: today
his face was snowing today
he rained mice

duplications and faint type
boxes checked and unchecked
pill counts rise and fall

faster through flipped pages
she flings the papers to shake
free his voice: *Mother!*

she is inches
from his face, feels
for his shoulders

he is centuries away
from his last
known address

Kristina Andersson Bicher

Credo

my songbird is a chill
in the desire
my sophistry a chimera
my soprano is a chimney
in the despair
my sorcerer is a chimpanzee
has no scruple
my sore is a chink
in the destination
my sorrow is a chip
in the destiny
my source is a choir
and is no longer miracle
has no smell
and is no longer misery
my speaker is a church
has no smile
my specialist is a cigarette
in the decimation
has no smoke
and is no longer missile
my species is a cinema
in the device
and is no longer mission
my son is a child
on an ice floe
has no skin
lonely
and no longer mine

Locked In

Men with glowstick wands slash and tilt
where they sent him.

After the incident with the steak knife
they were all given pills and circles to walk in—
staff admonished, sheriff summoned, utensils
sequestered.

Where they sent him, addicts
and loons are put in the woods, slop the pigs,
chop chop carry water
tap the trees and all be well.

There are 50 silver whirring ceiling fans for each man
where they sent him. The ceilings are 30 feet high
and they spin at the speed of thought.

The residents have no ballast and shuffle their clay feet
just enough to keep the building
from spinning up into space and the men
from becoming cut-loose kites.

Where they sent him, men live in glass houses
and are easy to break. It took three years
to find a dead body in the pond.

The men cannot wander off. There are sealed buses
for viewing reality, neon castles if you're good.

Kristina Andersson Bicher

Where they sent him, bedroom doors have no bolts
or latches and the doors
to the world are alarmed.

When He Calls

Every day the child calls from jail and
sometimes he's lonely
and asks after the animals: have they
forgotten him and do I
still love him and sometimes asks
for a lullaby.

Lazarus, I say, get up. The door
is unlocked.

Kristina Andersson Bicher

Refractory
an illness (esp. psychiatric) that does not respond to all known treatments

in another poem the boy was drowning
in another poem the mother was missing
in another poem someone else's mother would only shake out
the remnants and fold the blanket
into infinite neatness

boys falling from the sky:
*the first was found at 7:27 a.m. in the snowfield
behind the Corpus Christi school
the second was found near the train tracks*

refractory means so sorry ma'am we've done all we could
we've used up our science but here's this beautiful
word and the word is a birdcall in your brain
then you fall in love with the word and you take
it to bed with you every night

at night in the streets there are armies
of refractories their eyes are fly-eyes turned in on themselves

refractory means faceted into a mil-
lion cuts
they are fal-
ling
from the sky

refractory is a mother who can't stop
being

Heat, Sob, Lily

you blink and they go away and you blink and they come back
and you blink and they stay

in the earlier poem about the drowning the boy was always
going to drown now it's become about the mother

let me tell you what the mother must do:
the mother must bear the blame must make the change must
never bleed must save herself must pull the lever and fall
through the floor where the bodies of the other mothers
have piled up now

oh but I'm not dressed for a funeral I'm still in my housecoat

and the fathers the fathers just chop
wood the future is ringing: don't pick it up

Kristina Andersson Bicher

Loving Lazarus

that he is alive:

that though it be poor, food will enter
his face

that has mouth, that what is mouthshaped
may sometimes seem smile

that blinks green glass
that reason decouples
at the rate of question, divide

that we wait, watch
at the rate of kind

is he coming
or gone

that stand that sit that he

that head will fall

into my lap like loose stone
that softbreathing pelt

foot soldier of
faith and mechanics

that smell of still living
his hands dust storm and dirt water

that simple collision of feet

floor-clothes, the bed, boxes
piles crumbs cartons

that he has risked everything
by rising, by opening
lungs, reach

out a hand that he is alive
that he has walked through years, that this
might be good day, be best day, yes

Kristina Andersson Bicher

On the Island Where Venus

de Milo last saw her own arms,
I stole a dark fig from a heavy tree.
Counted 30 tiny goats eating up the hills.
My legs bobbed blue in the Aegean.
Mirrored sunglasses flashed where they fell among stones.
We laughed at what the American said.
The margaritas were bad & we drank them & laughed more.

The Minoans, we learned, were a good & gentle folk.
They were also short in stature.
When the Myceneans came along, their artwork grew swords.

Lazarus, today was mostly beautiful. Get up. I miss you.

Aftermath

and whether she is running a hand over her lover's chest or
 whether she is lifting
small weights, now left, now right, and counting by fives or

whether driving, whether wiping crumbs she is thinking my
 born child gone

whether rising at dusk or driving for milk, my known child
 missing. But who is this
here, in the shape of him: his shell and the scent of his voice,
 the eyes, yet dim, yet deep

a stare to rattle the rocks and uproot the sky and he will hand
 you things, broken
jewels he has rummaged for in his brain and his love is a dark
 leaf out of reach, he's

a foundering rock and you're a collapse

if you want to find him, look in the high green crowns of trees
 that ring the town

III.

Young Carl Jung

Young Carl Jung is dreaming again
in his painted bed:

Mother wears a skirt
made of cutlery
shingling out from her tiny middle.
She dips and swirls,
young Carl lunges
at the flash of ankles,
gets swept in circles across the floor.

He cries out *Vater!*
The archway darkens
with Martin Luther,
no, the Elf King.
Wait, it's Herr Doktor Freud
the father he's yet to meet:
three-piece tweed,
glint of chain, cigar cocked
in his right hand.

Mother wails, her skirt
flares open with the jangle
of a thousand cymbals.

Young Carl Jung is screaming again
in his painted bed:

Kristina Andersson Bicher

Ampersands & Runes—
Father, how you pocketwatch,
Mother, you're a spoon!

More to Say

Lately she wants to write stories. People
to show you: the elegant Dutch doctor, his red
dog, platinum attaché case, this pin oak
in a pose, that puckered kite, plus
all this bright weather. And there's more to say,
his wonderful shoes. She wants to make new
words … like *penipevorium*
instead of penis because his penis
deserves something grand.

In Amsterdam, Waiting

for dear Jack as he catches the last train from Eindhoven
to meet me—

I have eaten a clean & decent cheese; drank a dram of Bach.
Washed then wandered

into a waffled hotel robe. Reordered my legs on the many-
feathered pillows. Outside a baby grand flops on a meat hook.

A barge pulls the grey-green ribbon of its grief
along the canal. The carmine shutters

are the flared & fixed gills of a giant wooden fish. Your voice
a vine of church and stream. Ancient clocks whir

their tiny tambourines. Soon, we will be two racehorses
in the age of elephants.

Undressed

She peels the red plasticene boots
down past chapped calves and blue
ankle bones. Picks off the small stone

from the sole of her foot. Removes
breastplate and bodice, rests
tiara on the nightstand. Unclinks
her silver cuffs and climbs

into bed. Two pigeons' mad
coupling rackets the nearby airshaft.
Where is sleep. The lasso

on the floor twitches
the dart of its tail and her discarded
skirt is a lake of dented stars.
Her hair, dark veins.

New Year's Eve

                maybe if she reads a book, a brick

of a thing on her thighs, then maybe she won't feel night press its back into the bedroom wall, feel windows bend, won't hear wind thinning through bare pines, and she won't think of him—

                if she spends hours shopping for loveseats online, watching

shows about swapping homes in Bali or Berlin, rent vs. own, while he has his hand up someone's skirt—if only she could rise into her own forehead, turn her eyes inward, flat as coins

                if only she could keep reading *A Strangeness in My Mind*, with a woman

in a small house on a hill in the outskirts of Istanbul, purple headscarf, stirring a stew, roasting chickpeas whilst the village belle just sped off in a sleek black taxi having eloped with the wrong man

                then she will not think of new love already lost, how it will not be

him for her, hated, darling, and maybe this will be the year the heat kicks on when it's called
the year he cleaves to a bride, then maybe she will no longer dissolve   on street corners, search for what in passing faces

Desire

What's this scuttling

under the sheets?
Scorpion, scorpion, no

more meat than a shadow has meat

but what a hammer he wields.
Golden arachnid, all the ladies
stand in line

to see how you died— gorgeous
bones splayed on curiosity's

floor while he watches

with his compound eye.
Or did you see him first?

Hello trap—

a little stab, then the treacle,
little drips of death syrup in.

Did you draw your finger down

the curl of his spine? This articulated
amber leaf of antique design

Love Is a Rebel Bird

after *Carmen*

ACT I

Asshat's Abecedarian

To wit: cocaine can indeed result in
overdose, as can any blood-orgasm, O
riginal sin being what we pimp for. Now spit.
Exhaust, exhume, expunge it. Extirpate
all silvery taste of me, predatoré of
decent meat. Why call me any
other name than
rapier?

Home Girl Busts a Limerick

will I bucket to ash in your hands—
cleaned of still, flushed of scrub—
face the harden, strip the touch—
your pluck-throat, your down-mouth, your scream—
til your hands fall to ash in a bucket! Then tongue—
I will scrub you so clean I will scrub you so clean—
down your throat, may your tongue strip it hard—
(*harder still*, do you scream), flush your mouth—
May your face sear your hands where you touch it—

ACT II

Spurned Love, Spanish Dance

Only ever the *seguidilla* of you:
black bra straps like snakes like bones
and I'm weak as green wheat in June
with hungers like roots through stone.

Black bra straps like snakes like bones
hair and lips stain pink
with hungers like roots through stone.
To hold a seed of you is to sink.

Hair and lips stain pink:
which is to say never again
to hold a seed of you, to sink
into the heaven that is your bed.

Which is to say never again
weak as green wheat in June
in the heaven that is your bed
only ever the *seguidilla* of you—

Femme Fatale Pens Her Own Elegy

Chez mon ami, my sleeve frayed with grief and I was so hot for destruction.
O mio nescio, negligent, Russian roulette on a Wednesday.

I did not covet nor hunger nor giddy my loins in ascendance.
Harrowed and hammered I stapled my kisses upon you.

Cold, in fact, colder, the stars' invocation; so odious my ardor.
Hail me as hex queen, incarnadine, canticle, threnody, curse.

Click-click, then a grinding of wheels, now my chamber is empty.
No use divination nor oracle, this chamber's empty.

ACT III

The Chase, a Dance

still he pursues her
in the noodle shop the stairs
still he pursues her

all this she bears
peels the ring off the floor
in the noodle shop the stairs

tinsel from the dime-store
and rust in his teeth
peels the ring off the floor

his voice a dark street
bristling with flowers
and rust in his teeth

bees ravage the bowers
fear pricks the heart
bristling with flowers

from the very start
fear pricks the heart
still he pursues her
still he pursues her

ACT IV

Love is a ...

Mutinous thug un-
broken wolf-bird saboteur
profligate fowl.

You run yoked choked and bridled
right smack into his talons—

Her Ambivalence

> *What am I to myself that must be remembered?*
> —Robert Creeley

cascade of floss &gold
she could not ascend
slick scented river

because Rapunzel's braid
was built for others

she ever the dark
rosette of someone
else's desire

now, heaven
so blued   so far
nights   &nights

her song grows   the cord
lengthens   *be for me*
she says

and casts herself
into the air
&again   again

Kristina Andersson Bicher

Mannequins

after Isa Genzken

we   with no openings   then nothing
leaves our body   then only

there's a ringing in this skin

what rises of me
falls back down in my feet

how heavylight, emptyfull   i

who cannot send a letter
cannot fall on knees

who moved cannot tremble

and therefore my hands coatrack
receive to receive   therefore giant bowl

therefore furniture

with your hoof hand please
stroke my blue wig

[chink]   my shell

if i sing, how song pools
into hollow legs like sadness   where

HEAT, SOB, LILY

are my genitals

my hand gone missing
hair doesn't fit

shirt stained

there is no hearing in this
i, fetish

IV.

Ars Poetica

Because when she rolled away the stone, nothing.

Empty is the condition of holding every potentiality.

The cave filled—heat, light, sob, lily—poured in with force.

Till those beams were spent. Met in measure by the void.

Because the stone was the only thing holding back the world.

The stone did all that. It was a big stone. Because hunger
    is a vacuum.

How hard it was then, to move the stone. The thing between
    her and herself.

Kristina Andersson Bicher

The First Time I Saw Jesus

I was rent   in wet heave   my mind
  loose weave   and he flew

from a window high high   flew and then fell
onto my left hand   pretty face

in the cut glass of my ring   when first I saw
Jesus he   loved me weak   on knees

* * *

I have lain with that   day   clawed
covers   torn bones   looking

spilled   my body from its cage   *I do not believe
in you   I do not   in you*

have called him every   cry   curse   calamity supplication

every gesture I could summon   to plead with his hard
immaculate hard   corpse

* * *

I don't know   resurrection   but my own
father who had let me down had let me down

came back after death   as a fly   and was heavy
with buzz and fight   his flight stumbly   but he lived

by my shoulder that whole long winter and for
his company   I was   grateful

* * *

One day   the radio sang
I've got a friend   in Jesus   and some transfiguration

pierced my palm   I fevered and I wagged   my finger
at the window   at the ragged wind windshield

and the beyond   and I heard   a voice
say I will not   give up on you on you I will not

give up on you   and it was a voice   I had never
heard   I was talking to him   then I recoiled   and in the
     silence

that followed yes I recoiled

Kristina Andersson Bicher

How to Get Divorced

FOR 20 YEARS, swallow everything. Eat until you are the
 heaviest pillow on the bed. Then
eat three pills a day to stay alive

But first, watch your mother build row upon row of poppies.
 And when you are only
four she will tell you they are opium poppies and will lose her
 face in their black crowns

Also watch your father build a deck made of splinters and all
 summer run bare foot

The kitchen floor always fresh-swept. For the longest time no
 one yells

One night a fist will go through glass then a rush to the
 phone. (A black polished handset
is a club that can split a mother's lip to gush.) And now they
 are cleaved

Your father will be three hours late each Saturday to pick you
 up. On the highway, he will weave
and gesticulate to no one. Will forget to buy food

Your mother will grow on her own out of nothing

Your father is weak and suffers so beautifully, you will love
 him best

Heat, Sob, Lily

AND THEN when it's your turn you will marry your father.
    And never admit the match was bad.

And for 20 years, you will swallow everything, eat until you
    are the heaviest pillow on the bed. Eat
three pills a day to stay alive

You will be corpulent in your despair. Shrink from your
    friends. And they will let you go

Then in midlife, a friend dies. And her dying is long. A slow-
    leaking; wasting, wet
goodbyes. New blue blazers are purchased for the boys and
    funeral shoes

NOW you know what to do. You make a secret plan. You
    count up the coins and call the lawyer

And though you hate yourself for it you call the lawyer

Kristina Andersson Bicher

On Boxing Day

The sad ones walk the beach's beaten trail

A neighbor barefoot on the gravel path grasps the fingers
Of some new lover and we nod at each other

It's a gray Sunday. And you want something new, want to be new

A close friend wants a divorce and another and another
Hopes to slide into a second marriage and one tugs at the leash.

The fallen oak leaves are thorned. It's the day after Christmas.
    People seem lost

The trees are lost; they blossom in the snow. Cherries and
    crab apples breaking apart
There should be snow bees, you once said, that come out in
    winter, only

Black and fuzzy white instead of yellow. Wouldn't that be a sight

The Book of Hope

I.
The Book of Hope is striped with fear.
The Book of Hope starts
here:
> 6 hours without rest we kissed.
> A Wednesday. Then day sprung. Hello
> sleepwalker.

I was born a stranger to myself and this persisted.
I look in a mirror. I reach out a hand but only touch glass.

Hello sleepwalker. I've passed a life in glass.
I got angry with my attorney. I got angry with my therapist.
> Hello sleepwalker.
I got angry. Everyone says you look normal to me.

II.
You said: *On Friday, we'll talk about Saturday.* Hope is the
> longest distance between two points.

III.
This could all be yours, said the morning, said the open
window and birdsong
rushing in.

This   said the boy to the girl to the
dog to the sheets.
Yours.

IV.
Don't touch! me & my sorrows
but sorrow my touch sorrow my plate and grieve my fork
sword-swallow me this   *worsor   orrosw   roswor*

      (day swallows, night swallows)

sorrowful wrens drenching
in the grief-green hedge

oh roses of harrow, of wet-wetness, vines
of deplete   grieve my fork & sour plate, swallow
day swallow night   *wrosor sworro*

roses & the sorrowing stallions of night

The Book of Hope says open, says ease, says let me, says
let me shed the tears.

V.
*Are you sleeping? darling? can you feel it? remember how I spoke
    of the third thing? it's here. now in the room. the third
        thing. can you hear it?*

Was hope scratching its walls?

VI.
Tell me something beautied
tell me no one
    tonight
      will swing
        from gallows

The Book of Hope on hiatus.

VII.
because I would not stop for
because I would not
stop sadness not I

because sadness would not stop

VIII.
only the bitterblack fingers of memory and smoke that hold

the sadness of the shtetl, villagers and lords
the sadness of money (new rich, old rich)
the sadness of bridge and wet branch, and dishes deep in
    cupboards

IX.
When Kristina dreams of the plague: Yes, Venice has stopped its rotting but it streams historic into her open-mouthed sleep and she sucks deep ... the sheets twitch their veins, the walls all filigree and bisque ... she wishes hard to grown more skin! Don't let it in. Bolt the door, seal the cracks, Kristina is dreaming of the plague!

X.
The Book of Hope flutters in some moody rain-drenched mouth

a plangeny to beat, to pound out melancholic
how waves, how wings of wind, how wrought and wrung and
    when has the world ever not been perilous?

XI.
it was unbearable until it wasn't
it was impossible until it wasn't

my lover is talking
I'm thinking about licorice: black briny
drooling inky   my lover
still talking

Criss-Crossed

> *I start in the middle of a sentence and move*
> *both directions at once.*
> —John Coltrane

L, then, for lonely, loose-limbed lust & M
mercurial, manacle, mire. N is
    (I played this game with myself, a cold
    Saturday going round the reservoir)

nevertheless outpatient, onlooker with
an operatic kernel. Plain Jane or pixelated
jazz, an indolent queen querying her hotness.

Get smart. You, stained trinket and utterly
veined. Weary. Except, except,
every friend goes dark with your zeal.

I's angry. I's alone.

Kristina Andersson Bicher

That Night Jack Wanted Me

Spaghetti and wine, then bed
with Jack

who's trying to reach me   in my body
where I lay   estranged   and neither

of us could find me
(& I'm saying ~~body~~, saying
~~me & my~~)

I wanted him too, from the deep
where I lay
where my name clung to leaves   Once

I was not false, doubled, had a me
and knew it   but tonight suddenly   I'm only

name   which is to say idea

the idea of a head   welded
onto someone's bicycle

or a fish head
on a spear with the wind blowing

on my face
which ripples
with sun and my one eye is a moon

on the night Jack wanted me

In Bed in the Country

11 pm	quiet froth then voices ricochet trees sing a nobody-song
11:01 pm	the blue dot at mind's end becomes Sistine the house exhales
1:30 am	dreaming of sex in aubergine beds watching sharks in quaver tanks flooding rooms a rush to rescue emeralds
3:17 am	freight train cleaves the dark jagging silver thread coyote yelps rise to mid-elm
3:30 am	moon-stark
5:45 am	roosters shout *the humans are at it what-the-HELL what-the-HELL*

Kristina Andersson Bicher

In New York

I.
The woman
makes love to a wheel while
the man makes
love to his money. Hold on,

you say (about the last part). The image
is old, the metaphor strains. Okay,
there was no commingling
of his fleshed parts with paper or coin

and yet, it's true, she sang
subordination. She wore
a white flag.

II.
Him, wheels wheeling.

Gears of gain, and cogs, the man
examines the woman from across
the table. How
do I game thee—

Him, lighting up inside.

III.
Consider the wheel. Utile and sturdy. Full
of holes. Without holes, too hard
to turn. A well-considered machine.

What are the wheel's natural enemies? Gravity,
friction. A woman. A man in
motion stays in motion.

IV.
She sees him seeing her, and in his face, then,
sees herself where before was dark. The woman who
mistook her husband for a husband is
an easy mark. He is lighting up inside.

V.
Last night, she couldn't sleep, waiting for his ping. Last
night, she couldn't sleep because the number of dead
kept rising. The wheel and its holes being restless.

VI.
A man in money stays in money.

What do wheels and money have
in common? A certain indifference
to consequence. Both can steer
away. Cleanly.

The woman thought she was
making love to the man but it was only
the wheel.

VII.
Spokes; rim; void. No unnecessary
architecture. She loved the wheel.

VIII.
A wheel needs an axle to survive. A wheel needs an axle to
    survive.
May I?

IX.
The man was also myth, meaning shiny crown, meaning
his greatness bore repeating. Therefore

was she Audience (her superpower was Audience). Was
Chief Polisher, Chief Listener.

When an audience gets used up, you get white flag.
A white flag to polish with.

X.
What happens when a metaphor is used up? It falls
on its side and fills with a woman's tears, begins
to breed mosquitoes.

Kristina Andersson Bicher

When I Say I Love Art, I Mean

there's one hot inch between your
shoulder and mine on this tufted crescent gallery
couch. You say *gypsum*, I counter *gesso*, and brush

a wet hair from my lip. Yes, the song they're playing
is Portuguese and we agree, the three large center
paintings are shit. If we end up in Times Square,

neon green would stripe your hotel bed and our entwined
legs. But here we sit now at the Whitney, afloat between
Hoboken and the High Line. Skyscrapers in China

are made with holes for dragons to fly through and nothing's
propping up this fifth floor but an architect's dream. Here's
a game: which one of us is smarter, who rhymes

harder? *Artifice, awkwardness, precipice, carapace,*
the empty mouth will fill. Oh, we ogled the de Koonings,
flitted past the circus, but see us stand by the river

glass and simmer in late sun. The wall text was insipid:
don't tell me the artist cut the canvas like a sail or
thickened her pigments with green tea and rust. The wind

of the world wicks through us now, sweeping
our feet toward the door.

An Insomniac to Her Men

These heinous pillows I clutch aren't you!
Knots and bulges and drafts under the duvet—

Dan, I *loved* you! flawed and flimsy
begging for dregs

And you, Weekend Boy, your earnest
grappling and square bacon pan,
pastel boxers strung up like pennants

Mr. Nine Doors, Bragger Bill, Jean-Luc, The Wheel—
O, it is dark among these rocks

I repeat my litany, I miss
the old enmities, my exes

Because it is late, I seek out
      my savior … Sir Klonopin, where
        are your promises now (*one metamorphosis, two*
           metamorphosis …)

Oaths I swore were oaken. But see, I love my men
broke open

Kristina Andersson Bicher

They Will Enter

they find a way in   spiders
mice   the sugarbrown
beetles   up the tub
squeezed through
kitchen slits   floor-
board bucklings

holes I didn't know
I had   hungry
they come

*

the world means to enter me   all
its creatures

because I would not
open
they find a way

*

I keep it all
tidy
unpierceable
and still

*

I cannot touch them
after they die I must
bring in help   their bodies
overwhelm me

the serpent was ugly and turned
himself to red fruit
so that Eve would put her lips
on him

she desired not
the serpent   not the man
but to eat the world

she took the bite when
she knew her mouth as huge

Kristina Andersson Bicher

Birth

In the beginning was the wound. All stories start with a wound.

Acknowledgments

For my family whose love and strength made me. For my beautiful children, wise and bold.

With deep thanks to all who have provided feedback on my work but especially Carla Carlson, Kathleen Ossip, and Anthony Cappo. Their generosity, care, discernment, and thoughtfulness is everything to me.

I am grateful to Marc Vincenz for his continued belief in my work, as well as the readers and editors who have endorsed poems.

Poems from this manuscript have been published in the following journals with possible modifications and/or different titles.

AGNI: "Says Daughter"

American Journal of Poetry: "In the News," "The Lazarus Files," "Rendered Human," and "Midwinter Penance"

Burning House Press: "Chronicles of Lazarus," "When He Calls," "Loving Lazarus," "Birth," and "After the War"

Colorado Review: "The Book of Hope" and "The First Time I Saw Jesus"

First Literary Review–East: "Girl Learns to Speak"

Glass: A Journal of Poetry: "Mannequins"

Crab Creek Review: "Rebel Bride"

Hayden's Ferry Review: "Neighbor Girl to Mrs. G"

Juxtaprose: "Ars Poetica"

Lana Turner Journal: "Criss-Crossed" and "Joseph's Annunciation"

Ocean State Review: "Refractory"

One Pen: "Her Ambivalence"

Ovenbird: "In Amsterdam, Waiting"
Ploughshares: "Recall"
Plume Poetry: "How to Get Divorced" and "Boxing Day"
Redivider: "Girl"
The Night Heron Barks: "When I Say I Love Art, I Mean"
Women's Studies Quarterly: "How to Survive a Shipwreck"

About the Author

KRISTINA ANDERSSON BICHER is the author of *She-Giant in the Land of Here-We-Go-Again* (MadHat Press), as well as the translator of Swedish poet Marie Lundquist's full-length collection *I walk around gathering up my garden for the night* (Bitter Oleander Press).

Her poetry appears in such literary journals as *AGNI, Ploughshares, Hayden's Ferry, Plume, Denver Quarterly, Colorado Review,* and *Narrative*. Her translations and nonfiction have appeared in *The Atlantic, Brooklyn Rail, Harvard Review, Asymptote,* and *Writer's Chronicle*, among others.

She holds an MFA from Sarah Lawrence College.

www.ingramcontent.com/pod-product-compliance
Lightning Source LLC
Chambersburg PA
CBHW020336170426
43200CB00006B/407

Praise for *Heat, Sob, Lily*

There's furious beauty and inventive, hard-driving music ("not always blossomsweet but breathbrute") to be found in *Heat, Sob, Lily*. The scrupulous way Kristina Andersson Bicher maps a woman's reality, italicizing female savvy and defiance, in her galvanizing lyric bulletins brings to mind the lightning-fierce, self-mythologizing Sylvia Plath of "Lady Lazarus" and the on-fire early poems of Margaret Atwood, but Andersson Bicher is indeed her own resilient X-ray engineer and lucid magician of 21st-century truthtelling. A riveting book!
   —Cyrus Cassells, author of *Is There Room for Another Horse on Your Horse Ranch?*

"The doors / to the world are alarmed," and ever since reading Kristina Andersson Bicher's *Heat, Sob, Lily*, I keep expecting the world around me to klaxon, to become more exciting, scary and vibrant. I find myself repeating, "love is a dark leaf out of reach" as I curl with "hungers like roots through stone." These impressionistic, musical poems dance with the fragment as they hope and harrow and "say wild wooded / things rattling the leaf bin." This book invites us to journey through childhood, seduction and lust, marriage and divorce, parenthood, illness and loss, arriving, gloriously, to utter "there should be snow bees…that come out in winter, only." So stop reading this blurb, "put down / your fruit glosses and curling wands, pick up that pipe wrench" and read poems that staple their kisses upon you, while they light "the petite torches / to see where the wind comes from." *Heat, Sob, Lily* is a profound, dazzling and powerful book.
   —Christopher Citro, author of *If We Had a Lemon We'd Throw It and Call That the Sun*

Two couplets, in separate poems, mark the poles of Kristina Andersson Bicher's *Heat, Sob, Lily*. First "it was unbearable until it wasn't / it was impossible until it wasn't" tells of the agony and helplessness a mother feels facing extreme circumstances. Then "Oaths I swore were oaken. But see, I love my men / broke open" explores the complications of desire. This is a book full of falls and slides: a set of keys into snow, a dog into a basement, the infant Jesus from heaven, and, of course, from innocence into experience. The poems possess startling candor and enormous subtlety. Finally we are told "I will not   give up on you on you I will not / give up on you and it was a voice   I had never / heard." This voice is the mother to the child, the Divine to the speaker, any of us to ourselves.

—Kathleen Ossip, author of *July*